This book belongs to:

....

....

....

....

For information about reusing material, cover image, or other images from this work, please write:

Permissions
The Christian Science Board of Directors
C/o The Writings of Mary Baker Eddy
One Norway Street, Boston, Massachusetts 02115, USA
Email: permissions@twmbe.com

Illustrations by Diane W. Allison

Library of Congress Control Number: 2007934994
ISBN: 978-0-87952-331-2 English
ISBN: 978-0-87952-332-9 Spanish

Printed in Hong Kong 2007

KF0709007A

Big with Blessings

Words by Mary Baker Eddy

Published by The Christian Science Board of Directors

Distributed by The Christian Science Publishing Society
Boston, Massachusetts, United States of America

This book is lovingly dedicated to
children around the world.

TO those leaning on
the sustaining infinite,
to-day is big with blessings.

The Lord's Prayer
with its Spiritual Interpretation

Our Father which art in heaven,
   Our Father-Mother God, all-harmonious,

Hallowed be Thy name.
   Adorable One.

Thy kingdom come.
   Thy kingdom is come; Thou art ever-present.

Thy will be done in earth, as it is in heaven.
   Enable us to know, — as in heaven, so on earth,
   — God is omnipotent, supreme.

Give us this day our daily bread;
   Give us grace for to-day;
   feed the famished affections;

And forgive us our debts, as we forgive our debtors.
   And Love is reflected in love;

And lead us not into temptation,
but deliver us from evil;
   And God leadeth us not into temptation,
   but delivereth us from sin, disease, and death.

For Thine is the kingdom, and the power,
and the glory, forever.
   For God is infinite, all-power, all Life, Truth,
   Love, over all, and All.

A Verse
for the Big Children

Father-Mother good, lovingly
    Thee I seek, —
      Patient, meek,
In the way Thou hast, —
Be it slow or fast,
    Up to Thee.

WHEN we wait patiently on God and seek Truth righteously, He directs our path.

"Feed My Sheep"

Shepherd, show me how to go
    O'er the hillside steep,
How to gather, how to sow, —
    How to feed Thy sheep;
I will listen for Thy voice,
    Lest my footsteps stray;
I will follow and rejoice
    All the rugged way.

Thou wilt bind the stubborn will,
    Wound the callous breast,
Make self-righteousness be still,
    Break earth's stupid rest.
Strangers on a barren shore,
    Lab'ring long and lone,
We would enter by the door,
    And Thou know'st Thine own;

So, when day grows dark and cold,
    Tear or triumph harms,
Lead Thy lambkins to the fold,
    Take them in Thine arms;
Feed the hungry, heal the heart,
    Till the morning's beam;
White as wool, ere they depart,
    Shepherd, wash them clean.

GOOD thoughts are an impervious armor; clad therewith you are completely shielded from the attacks of error of every sort. And not only yourselves are safe, but all whom your thoughts rest upon are thereby benefited.

THUS founded upon the rock of Christ, when storm and tempest beat against this sure foundation, you, safely sheltered in the strong tower of hope, faith, and Love, are God's nestlings; and He will hide you in His feathers till the storm has passed. Into His haven of Soul there enters no element of earth to cast out angels, to silence the right intuition which guides you safely home.

The Daily Prayer

"Thy kingdom come;"
let the reign of divine Truth, Life,
and Love be established in me,
and rule out of me all sin;
and may Thy Word
enrich the affections of all
mankind, and govern them!

WHEN angels visit us,
we do not hear the rustle of wings,
nor feel the feathery touch
of the breast of a dove;
but we know their presence
by the love they create in our hearts.
Oh, may you feel *this* touch, —
it is not the clasping of hands,
nor a loved person present;
it is more than this:
it is a spiritual idea that lights your path!

The Twenty-Third Psalm with its Spiritual Sense

[DIVINE LOVE] is my shepherd; I shall not want.

[LOVE] maketh me to lie down in green pastures: [LOVE] leadeth me beside the still waters.

[LOVE] restoreth my soul [spiritual sense]: [LOVE] leadeth me in the paths of righteousness for His name's sake.

Yea, though I walk through the valley of the shadow of death, I will fear no evil: for [LOVE] is with me; [LOVE'S] rod and [LOVE'S] staff they comfort me.

[LOVE] prepareth a table before me in the presence of mine enemies: [LOVE] anointeth my head with oil; my cup runneth over.

Surely goodness and mercy shall follow me all the days of my life; and I will dwell in the house [the consciousness] of [LOVE] for ever.

The Scientific Statement of Being

There is no life, truth, intelligence, nor substance in matter.
All is infinite Mind and its infinite manifestation,
for God is All-in-all.
Spirit is immortal Truth;
matter is mortal error.
Spirit is the real and eternal;
matter is the unreal and temporal.
Spirit is God, and man is His image and likeness.
Therefore man is not material; he is spiritual.

GOD fashions all things, after His own likeness.
Life is reflected in existence,
Truth in truthfulness, God in goodness,
which impart their own peace and permanence.

LOVE

Brood o'er us with Thy shelt'ring wing,
   'Neath which our spirits blend
Like brother birds, that soar and sing,
   And on the same branch bend.
The arrow that doth wound the dove
Darts not from those who watch and love.

If thou the bending reed wouldst break
   By thought or word unkind,
Pray that his spirit you partake,
   Who loved and healed mankind:
Seek holy thoughts and heavenly strain,
That make men one in love remain.

Learn, too, that wisdom's rod is given
   For faith to kiss, and know;
That greetings glorious from high heaven,
   Whence joys supernal flow,
Come from that Love, divinely near,
Which chastens pride and earth-born fear,

Through God, who gave that word of might
   Which swelled creation's lay:
"Let there be light, and there was light."
   What chased the clouds away?
'Twas Love whose finger traced aloud
A bow of promise on the cloud.

Thou to whose power our hope we give,
   Free us from human strife.
Fed by Thy love divine we live,
   For Love alone is Life;
And life most sweet, as heart to heart
Speaks kindly when we meet and part.

CHILDREN. The spiritual thoughts and
representatives of Life, Truth, and Love....

JESUS loved little children because of their freedom
from wrong and their receptiveness of right.

PRACTICE not profession,
understanding not belief,
gain the ear and right hand
of omnipotence
and they assuredly call
down infinite blessings.

GOD expresses in man
the infinite idea
forever developing itself,
broadening and rising
higher and higher
from a boundless basis.

BE "of one mind," "in one place,"
and God will pour you out a blessing
such as you never before received.
He who dwelleth in eternal light
is bigger than the shadow,
and will guard and guide His own.

WHEN the
destination is
desirable,
expectation
speeds our
progress.

Satisfied

It matters not what be thy lot,
    So Love doth guide;
For storm or shine, pure peace is thine,
    Whate'er betide.

And of these stones, or tyrants' thrones,
    God able is
To raise up seed — in thought and deed —
    To faithful His.

Aye, darkling sense, arise, go hence!
    Our God is good.
False fears are foes — truth tatters those,
    When understood.

Love looseth thee, and lifteth me,
    Ayont hate's thrall:
There Life is light, and wisdom might,
    And God is All.

The centuries break, the earth-bound wake,
    God's glorified!
Who doth His will — His likeness still —
    Is satisfied.

BELOVED children, the world has need of you, — and more as children than as men and women: it needs your innocence, unselfishness, faithful affection, uncontaminated lives. You need also to watch, and pray that you preserve these virtues unstained, and lose them not through contact with the world. What grander ambition is there than to maintain in yourselves what Jesus loved, and to know that your example, more than words, makes morals for mankind!

The Sixth Tenet

And we solemnly promise to watch, and pray for that Mind to be in us which was also in Christ Jesus; to do unto others as we would have them do unto us; and to be merciful, just, and pure.

HOME is the dearest spot on earth, and it should be the centre, though not the boundary, of the affections.

DIVINE presence, breathe Thou
Thy blessing on every heart in
this house.

GRATITUDE and love should abide in
every heart each day of all the years.

HAPPINESS consists in being and in doing good; only what God gives, and what we give ourselves and others through His tenure, confers happiness: conscious worth satisfies the hungry heart, and nothing else can.

WHATEVER furnishes the semblance of an idea governed by its Principle, furnishes food for thought. Through astronomy, natural history, chemistry, music, mathematics, thought passes naturally from effect back to cause.

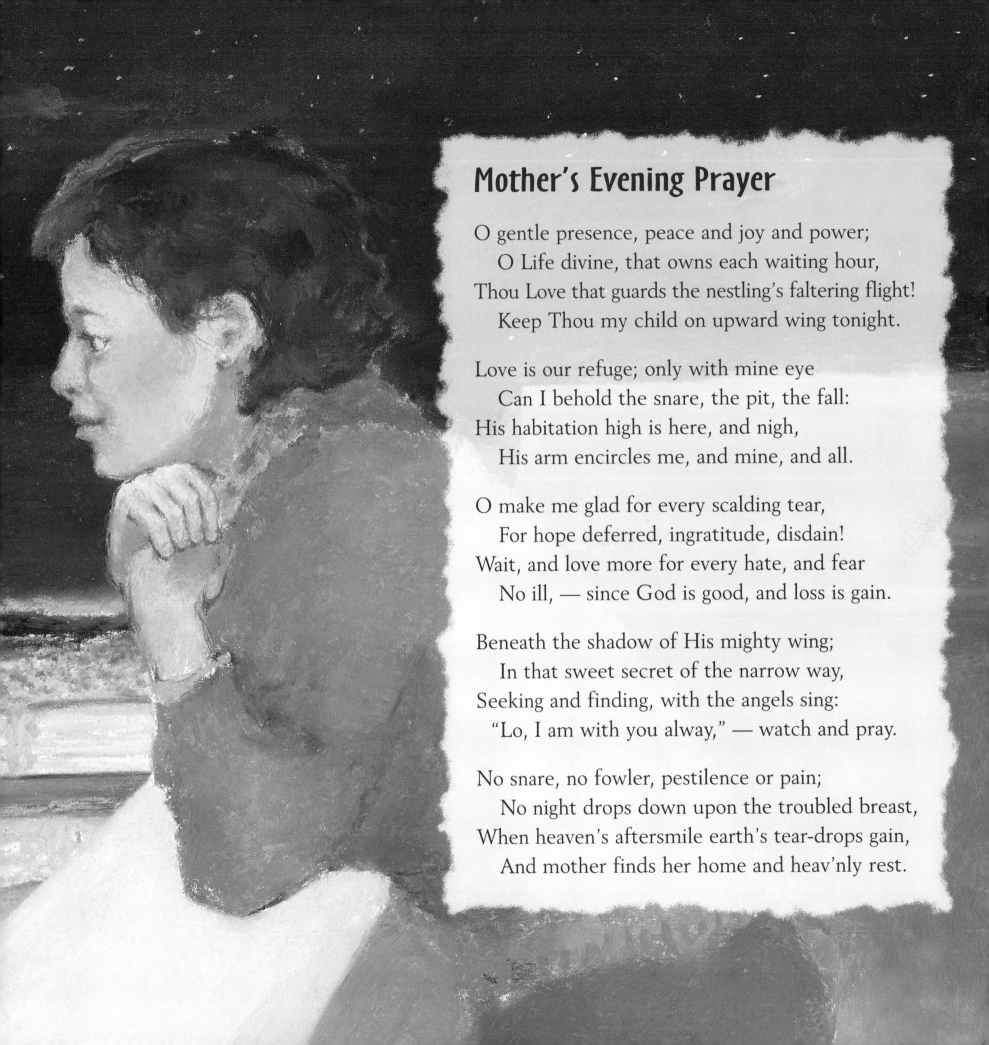

Mother's Evening Prayer

O gentle presence, peace and joy and power;
   O Life divine, that owns each waiting hour,
Thou Love that guards the nestling's faltering flight!
   Keep Thou my child on upward wing tonight.

Love is our refuge; only with mine eye
   Can I behold the snare, the pit, the fall:
His habitation high is here, and nigh,
   His arm encircles me, and mine, and all.

O make me glad for every scalding tear,
   For hope deferred, ingratitude, disdain!
Wait, and love more for every hate, and fear
   No ill, — since God is good, and loss is gain.

Beneath the shadow of His mighty wing;
   In that sweet secret of the narrow way,
Seeking and finding, with the angels sing:
   "Lo, I am with you alway," — watch and pray.

No snare, no fowler, pestilence or pain;
   No night drops down upon the troubled breast,
When heaven's aftersmile earth's tear-drops gain,
   And mother finds her home and heav'nly rest.

A Verse
for the Little Children

Father-Mother God,
    Loving me, —
Guard me when I sleep;
Guide my little feet
    Up to Thee.

Below, you can find this book's quotations with their citations in their entirety. If you're looking for deeper study into Mary Baker Eddy's writings, these quotes and poems are a great jumping off point into her various books.

TO those leaning on the sustaining infinite, to-day is big with blessings. (*Science and Health with Key to the Scriptures*, vii:1-2)

The Lord's Prayer with its Spiritual Interpretation

Our Father which art in heaven,
Our Father-Mother God, all-harmonious,

Hallowed be Thy name.
Adorable One.

Thy kingdom come.
Thy kingdom is come; Thou art ever-present.

Thy will be done in earth, as it is in heaven.
Enable us to know, — as in heaven, so on earth,
— God is omnipotent, supreme.

Give us this day our daily bread;
Give us grace for to-day;
feed the famished affections;

And forgive us our debts, as we forgive our debtors.
And Love is reflected in love;

And lead us not into temptation,
but deliver us from evil;
And God leadeth us not into temptation,
but delivereth us from sin, disease, and death.

For Thine is the kingdom, and the power,
and the glory, forever.
For God is infinite, all-power, all Life, Truth,
Love, over all, and All.
(*Science and Health*, 16:26-15)

A Verse for the Big Children

Father-Mother good, lovingly
    Thee I seek, —
    Patient, meek,
In the way Thou hast, —
Be it slow or fast,
    Up to Thee.
(*Miscellaneous Writings 1883-1896*, 400:19-25 and *Poems*, 69:7)

WHEN we wait patiently on God and seek Truth righteously, He directs our path. (*Science and Health*, 254:10-12)

"Feed My Sheep"

Shepherd, show me how to go
    O'er the hillside steep,
How to gather, how to sow, —
    How to feed Thy sheep;
I will listen for Thy voice,
    Lest my footsteps stray;
I will follow and rejoice
    All the rugged way.

Thou wilt bind the stubborn will,
    Wound the callous breast,
Make self-righteousness be still,
    Break earth's stupid rest.
Strangers on a barren shore,
    Lab'ring long and lone,
We would enter by the door,
    And Thou know'st Thine own;

So, when day grows dark and cold,
    Tear or triumph harms,
Lead Thy lambkins to the fold,
    Take them in Thine arms;
Feed the hungry, heal the heart,
    Till the morning's beam;
White as wool, ere they depart,
    Shepherd, wash them clean.
(*Miscellaneous Writings*, 397:21-20 and *Poems*, 14:1)

GOOD thoughts are an impervious armor; clad therewith you are completely shielded from the attacks of error of every sort. And not only yourselves are safe, but all whom your thoughts rest upon are thereby benefited.
(*The First Church of Christ, Scientist, and Miscellany*, 210:7)

THUS founded upon the rock of Christ, when storm and tempest beat against this sure foundation, you, safely sheltered in the strong tower of hope, faith, and Love, are God's nestlings; and He will hide you in His feathers till the storm has passed. Into His haven of Soul there enters no element of earth to cast out angels, to silence the right intuition which guides you safely home. (*Miscellaneous Writings*, 152:22)

The Daily Prayer

"Thy kingdom come;" let the reign of divine Truth, Life, and Love be established in me, and rule out of me all sin; and may Thy Word enrich the affections of all mankind, and govern them! (*Manual of The Mother Church*, 41:21)

WHEN angels visit us, we do not hear the rustle of wings, nor feel the feathery touch of the breast of a dove; but we know their presence by the love they create in our hearts. Oh, may you feel *this* touch, — it is not the clasping of hands, nor a loved person present; it is more than this: it is a spiritual idea that lights your path!
(*Miscellaneous Writings*, 306:23-28)

The Twenty-Third Psalm with its Spiritual Sense

[DIVINE LOVE] is my shepherd; I shall not want.

[LOVE] maketh me to lie down in green pastures: [LOVE] leadeth me beside the still waters.

[LOVE] restoreth my soul [spiritual sense]: [LOVE] leadeth me in the paths of righteousness for His name's sake.

Yea, though I walk through the valley of the shadow of death, I will fear no evil: for [LOVE] is with me; [LOVE'S] rod and [LOVE'S] staff they comfort me.

[LOVE] prepareth a table before me in the presence of mine enemies: [LOVE] anointeth my head with oil; my cup runneth over.

Surely goodness and mercy shall follow me all the days of my life; and I will dwell in the house [the consciousness] of [LOVE] for ever.
(*Science and Health*, 578:4-18)

The Scientific Statement of Being

There is no life, truth, intelligence, nor substance in matter. All is infinite Mind and its infinite manifestation, for God is All-in-all. Spirit is immortal Truth; matter is mortal error. Spirit is the real and eternal; matter is the unreal and temporal. Spirit is God, and man is His image and likeness. Therefore man is not material; he is spiritual. (*Science and Health*, 468:8-15)

GOD fashions all things, after His own likeness. Life is reflected in existence, Truth in truthfulness, God in goodness, which impart their own peace and permanence.
(*Science and Health*, 516:9-12)

LOVE

Brood o'er us with Thy shelt'ring wing,
    'Neath which our spirits blend
Like brother birds, that soar and sing,
    And on the same branch bend.
The arrow that doth wound the dove
Darts not from those who watch and love.

If thou the bending reed wouldst break
    By thought or word unkind,
Pray that his spirit you partake,
    Who loved and healed mankind:
Seek holy thoughts and heavenly strain,
That make men one in love remain.

Learn, too, that wisdom's rod is given
    For faith to kiss, and know;
That greetings glorious from high heaven,
    Whence joys supernal flow,
Come from that Love, divinely near,
Which chastens pride and earth-born fear,

Through God, who gave that word of might
    Which swelled creation's lay:
"Let there be light, and there was light."
    What chased the clouds away?
'Twas Love whose finger traced aloud
A bow of promise on the cloud.

Thou to whose power our hope we give,
    Free us from human strife.
Fed by Thy love divine we live,
    For Love alone is Life;
And life most sweet, as heart to heart
Speaks kindly when we meet and part.
(*Miscellaneous Writings*, 387:7-12 (next page) and *Poems*, 6:1)

CHILDREN. The spiritual thoughts and representatives of Life, Truth, and Love.... (*Science and Health*, 582:28)

JESUS loved little children because of their freedom from wrong and their receptiveness of right. (*Science and Health*, 236:28-29)

PRACTICE not profession, understanding not belief, gain the ear and right hand of omnipotence and they assuredly call down infinite blessings.   (*Science and Health*, 15:28-30)

GOD expresses in man the infinite idea forever developing itself, broadening and rising higher and higher from a boundless basis. (*Science and Health*, 258:13-15)

BE "of one mind," "in one place," and God will pour you out a blessing such as you never before received. He who dwelleth in eternal light is bigger than the shadow, and will guard and guide His own. (*Miscellaneous Writings*, 134:12)

WHEN the destination is desirable, expectation speeds our progress. (*Science and Health*, 426:8-9)

Satisfied

It matters not what be thy lot,
    So Love doth guide;
For storm or shine, pure peace is thine,
    Whate'er betide.

And of these stones, or tyrants' thrones,
    God able is
To raise up seed — in thought and deed —
    To faithful His.

Aye, darkling sense, arise, go hence!
    Our God is good.
False fears are foes — truth tatters those,
    When understood.

Love looseth thee, and lifteth me,
    Ayont hate's thrall:
There Life is light, and wisdom might,
    And God is All.

The centuries break, the earth-bound wake,
    God's glorified!
Who doth His will — His likeness still —
    Is satisfied.
(*Poems*, 79:1)

BELOVED children, the world has need of you, — and more as children than as men and women: it needs your innocence, unselfishness, faithful affection, uncontaminated lives. You need also to watch, and pray that you preserve these virtues unstained, and lose them not through contact with the world. What grander ambition is there than to maintain in yourselves what Jesus loved, and to know that your example, more than words, makes morals for mankind! (*Miscellaneous Writings*, 110:4)

The Sixth Tenet

And we solemnly promise to watch, and pray for that Mind to be in us which was also in Christ Jesus; to do unto others as we would have them do unto us; and to be merciful, just, and pure. (*Science and Health*, 497:24)

HOME is the dearest spot on earth, and it should be the centre, though not the boundary, of the affections. (*Science and Health*, 58:21)

DIVINE presence, breathe Thou Thy blessing on every heart in this house. (*Pulpit and Press*, 10:27-28)

GRATITUDE and love should abide in every heart each day of all the years. (*Manual of The Mother Church*, 60:15-17)

HAPPINESS consists in being and in doing good; only what God gives, and what we give ourselves and others through His tenure, confers happiness: conscious worth satisfies the hungry heart, and nothing else can. (*Message to The Mother Church, 1902*, 17:22-25)

WHATEVER furnishes the semblance of an idea governed by its Principle, furnishes food for thought. Through astronomy, natural history, chemistry, music, mathematics, thought passes naturally from effect back to cause. (*Science and Health*, 195:15)

Mother's Evening Prayer

O gentle presence, peace and joy and power;
    O Life divine, that owns each waiting hour,
Thou Love that guards the nestling's faltering flight!
    Keep Thou my child on upward wing tonight.

Love is our refuge; only with mine eye
    Can I behold the snare, the pit, the fall:
His habitation high is here, and nigh,
    His arm encircles me, and mine, and all.

O make me glad for every scalding tear,
    For hope deferred, ingratitude, disdain!
Wait, and love more for every hate, and fear
    No ill, — since God is good, and loss is gain.

Beneath the shadow of His mighty wing;
    In that sweet secret of the narrow way,
Seeking and finding, with the angels sing:
    "Lo, I am with you alway," — watch and pray.

No snare, no fowler, pestilence or pain;
    No night drops down upon the troubled breast,
When heaven's aftersmile earth's tear-drops gain,
    And mother finds her home and heav'nly rest.
(*Miscellaneous Writings*, 389:5-25 and *Poems*, 4:1)

A Verse for the Little Children

Father-Mother God,
    Loving me, —
Guard me when I sleep;
Guide my little feet
    Up to Thee.
(*Miscellaneous Writings*, 400:13-18
and *Poems*, 69:1)